P is for Peach

A Georgia Alphabet

Written by Carol Crane
Illustrated by Mark Braught

Sleeping Bear Press
310 North Main Street
Suite 300
Chelsea, MI 48118
www.sleepingbearpress.com

Printed and bound in Canada.

10 9 8 7 6 5 4 3 2

Library of Congress Cataloging-in-Publication Data

Crane, Carol, 1933-
P is for peach : a Georgia alphabet / by Carol Crane ; illustrated
by Mark Braught.
p. cm.
Summary: Information about the state of Georgia is presented in an
alphabetical arrangement.
ISBN 1-58536-046-5
1. Georgia—Juvenile literature. 2. English language—Alphabet—
Juvenile literature. [1. Georgia. 2. Alphabet.] I. Title: Georgia alphabet.
 II. Braught, Mark, ill. III. Title.
F286.3 .C73 2002
975.8—dc21
2002004302

Carol Crane

Lecturer and book reviewer Carol Crane is widely recognized by many schools and educators for her expertise in children's literature. She has conducted in-service seminars for teachers at many schools across the country. Eight years ago, Carol instituted a summer reading program for teachers and media specialists.

P is for Peach is Carol's sixth book with Sleeping Bear Press. She has also authored *P is for Palmetto: A South Carolina Alphabet*; *L is for Last Frontier: An Alaska Alphabet*; *L is for Lone Star: A Texas Alphabet*; *Sunny Numbers: A Florida Counting Book*, and *S is for Sunshine: A Florida Alphabet*. She travels extensively and speaks at state reading conventions across the United States.

Mark Braught

Mark Braught's 25 years of professional experience have earned him prestigious awards from The American Advertising Federation (ADDY), *Communication Arts*, the NY Art Directors Club, and the Society of Illustrators among others. He received his degree in graphic design from Indiana State University, and attended the Minneapolis College of Art & Design. He lives in Commerce, Georgia, with his wife Laura, five cats, and Charlie the dog.

Reference List

Barr, Tom. 1995. *Unique Georgia*. Santa Fe, New Mexico: John Muir Publications.

Couch, Ernie and Jill. 1993. *Georgia Trivia*. Nashville, Tennessee: Rutledge Hills Press.

Dalton Chamber of Commerce [Online]. www.daltonchamber.org [Accessed 2002].

Dalton History [Online]. www.northga.net/whitfield/dltnhis.html. [Accessed 2002].

Groene, Janet and Gordon. 1996. *Natural Wonders of Georgia*. Oaks, Pennsylvania: Country Roads Press

Kunerth, Jeff and Melvin, Don. 1997. *Georgia Adventure*. Nashville, Tennessee: Rutledge Hills Press.

Martin, Suzanne. 1999. *Awesome Almanac Georgia*. Walworth, Wisconsin: B & B Publishing, Inc.

Schemmel, William. 1999. *Georgia: Off the Beaten Path*. Old Saybrook, Connecticut: The Globe Pequot Press.

Shangle, Robert D. 1991. *Images of Georgia*. Portland, Oregon: LTA Publishing Company.

Stann, Kap. 1999. *Georgia Handbook*. Chico, California: Moon Travel Handbooks.

Stone Mountain Park [Online]. www.stonemountainpark.com/general/. [Accessed 2002].

Zweifel, Karyn K. 1998. *Gorgeous Georgia*. Nashville, Tennessee: Premium Press America.

A Bushel of Peachy Facts

1. In 1821, Chief Sequoya developed an 86-character Cherokee alphabet which was called what?

2. What is manufactured in Georgia that many schoolchildren ride on every day?

3. Providence Canyon with cliffs, peaks, and edges of orange, yellow, purple, gray, and red has been call Georgia's what?

4. What are the two longest rivers in Georgia?

5. Forests cover more than two-thirds of Georgia. What products does the slash pine provide?

6. What famous gunfighter and gambler grew up in the city of Valdosta?

7. Waycross and Okefenokee Swamp are the homes of what cartoon opossum?

8. Gainesville is the center for what two products that lead the nation in sales?

9. What is mayhaw?

10. What is the name of the fruitcake company that sells more than six million pounds of cake a year?

11. What famous blind singer from Georgia sings the official state song as his theme song?

12. Spanish missions and many forts were built of what material unique to the southern coast?

13. What name was given to the famous baseball player Ty Cobb?

14. Dr. Crawford W. Long, born in Danielsville, Georgia, made medical history when he used what as an anesthesia?

15. What is the name of the longest covered bridge in Georgia?

16. In 1970, what famous circus performer walked across a 1,000 foot long tightrope stretched 750 feet above Tallulah Gorge, in northeast Georgia?

17. What is the state fish of Georgia?

18. In 1793, what man invented the cotton gin?

19. What famous document did Georgians Button Gwinnett, Lyman Hall, and George Walton sign in 1776?

20. What city is still known today as "The South's Oldest Industrial City"?

21. William Howard Taft, 27th president of the United States, needed what from Barnesville, Georgia?

22. Savannah has cobblestone streets along its waterfront. Where did they come from?

23. The state's biggest and most "official" pig-cooking contest is called what?

24. What brightly colored, red, blue, and yellow-green bird may be seen along the coastal regions in the summer?

Joel Chandler Harris was born in Eatonton, Georgia. He lived in a small house near a plantation. It was on the plantation that he would sit and listen to the stories that were authentic African-American folklore, wonderful stories of Brer Rabbit, Brer Fox, and the other creatures who lived and pulled tricks along the Big Road. Mr. Harris later wrote about Uncle Remus, who told these stories of the American South. Many of Harris's writings were articles written for newspapers. In 1880 his book *Uncle Remus: His Songs and Sayings* was a best-seller. He wrote 185 tales in nearly thirty years of writing. One of his good friends was fellow author Mark Twain.

In 1946, Walt Disney produced a wonderful movie called *Song of the South*. Based on Harris's collection of stories, the movie won many awards and the song "Zip-A-Dee-Doo-Dah" won an Oscar.

Z is for "Zip-A-Dee-Doo-Dah," a Disney movie's catchy song. Taken from tales by Joel Chandler Harris, just tap your toes and sing along.

HARRIS

Aa

A is for Atlanta.
It is the capital of our state.
Gold dome we see from afar,
where rules and laws we legislate.

The citizens of Dahlonega, Georgia, gave the state a gift of gold in 1958. The precious gold was pounded into sheets and then attached to the dome of the capitol. As years went by the gold flaked and peeled off. Again, the school children and citizens of Dahlonega collected money for gold to gild the capitol dome. Today this gold dome is a shiny greeting for all to see. Miss Freedom, a statue on top of the dome, is 15 feet tall and weighs 2,000 pounds.

Atlanta is home to many famous people, businesses, and historical events. Some of them are: Martin Luther King Jr. National Historic Site; the World of Coca-Cola; Cable News Network (CNN); Underground Atlanta, which has existed since the Civil War; and Zoo Atlanta.

The brown thrasher's verse sounds like, "*plant-a-seed, plant-a-seed; drop it, drop it; cover-it-up, cover-it-up; eat-it-all, eat-it-all; chew-it, chew-it.*" He also makes loud smacks, hisses, and clicks. He has a reddish brown back, heavily streaked whitish underparts that have a buff color on the sides and breast, and yellow eyes. A long curved bill, long tail, and streaked underparts make it different than other thrushes. The mother bird lays three to five pale bluish-white eggs, which are covered with reddish-brown marks. Mother and father bird share nest-building and sitting on the eggs.

B b

B is for the Brown thrasher,
our state's official bird.
Its voice repeats a verse
I think you might have heard.

C is for the Cherokee rose,
a gold center in a ring of pure white.
It is the official flower of our state,
representing the Cherokee mothers' plight.

In 1838, after gold was discovered on Cherokee land, the tribe was sent to Oklahoma by order of President Andrew Jackson. The trail was long and hard, especially for mothers with their children. It became known as the Trail of Tears. A legend is told that a beautiful rose grew along the trail to lift the spirits of the sad mothers. Wherever a tear fell to the ground, a rose grew. The gold center of the rose stands for the gold taken from the Cherokee lands. Seven leaves on the stem of the flower represent the seven Cherokee clans that made the journey.

In 1979, the azalea was chosen as Georgia's state wildflower. When riding along mountain roads or busy highways, this flower with bright colored blossoms welcomes us.

C

Dd

Now, **D** is for Dalton,
where the carpeting industry began.
Started by a Georgia woman,
tufting and selling bedspreads with a plan.

A worldwide carpet industry grew from the creation of a simple wedding gift. Catherine Evans Whitener was just a teenager in 1895 when she thought to use an old technique—hand-tufted embroidery known as candlewick—to make a bedspread as a gift. A family friend saw the bedspread and paid Catherine to make another one like it. Demand for the bedspreads grew into the early twentieth century and Catherine began involving other local women to help her make more. An entire tufting industry grew out of this demand and helped many Georgia families survive through the Depression.

The most popular way to buy a bedspread was along U.S. Highway 41, where they were hung out on clotheslines to dry. This stretch of highway became known as "Bedspread" or "Peacock" Alley, after one of the more popular patterns. After World War II, new machines made the tufting process easier and production shifted from spreads to rugs. Dalton has remained on top as the world's largest carpet manufacturer, producing more than 80% of America's carpeting.

E e

Some of Georgia's early Native Americans were mound builders. They built huge mounds of earth with flat tops and used them for temples or burial grounds. The largest of these mounds is 63 feet tall and covers three acres.

The mound builders were great artists. Many necklaces and earrings of shell, copper, and feathers have been found, as well as stone statues. They traded with other tribes using the Etowah River to travel to New Orleans in the south, and samples of their work have been found as far north as Wisconsin. These mounds are a reminder of Georgia's early history. You can visit them in Cartersville.

E is for the Etowah Indian Mounds,
a symbol of Native Americans from long ago.
They lived and traveled afar,
on rivers meeting other tribes they did not know.

F is for the Fernbank Science Center.
It was one family's dream—
a school where children can learn,
in a forest and science theme.